Bullshit Story

Adorable Swear Word To Color

FOR STRESS RELEASING

By

Cathy Chadison

Happy Coloring

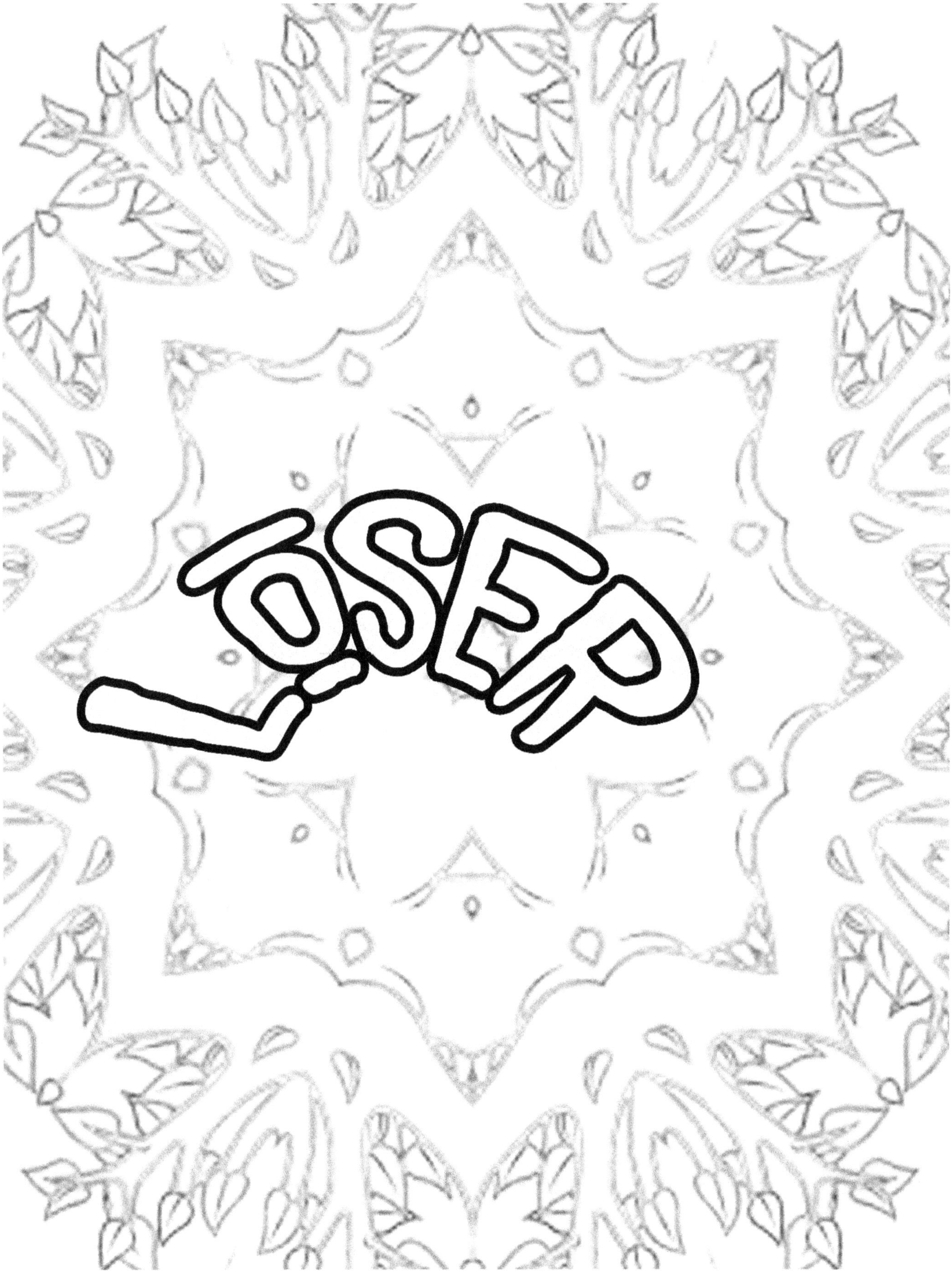
LOSER

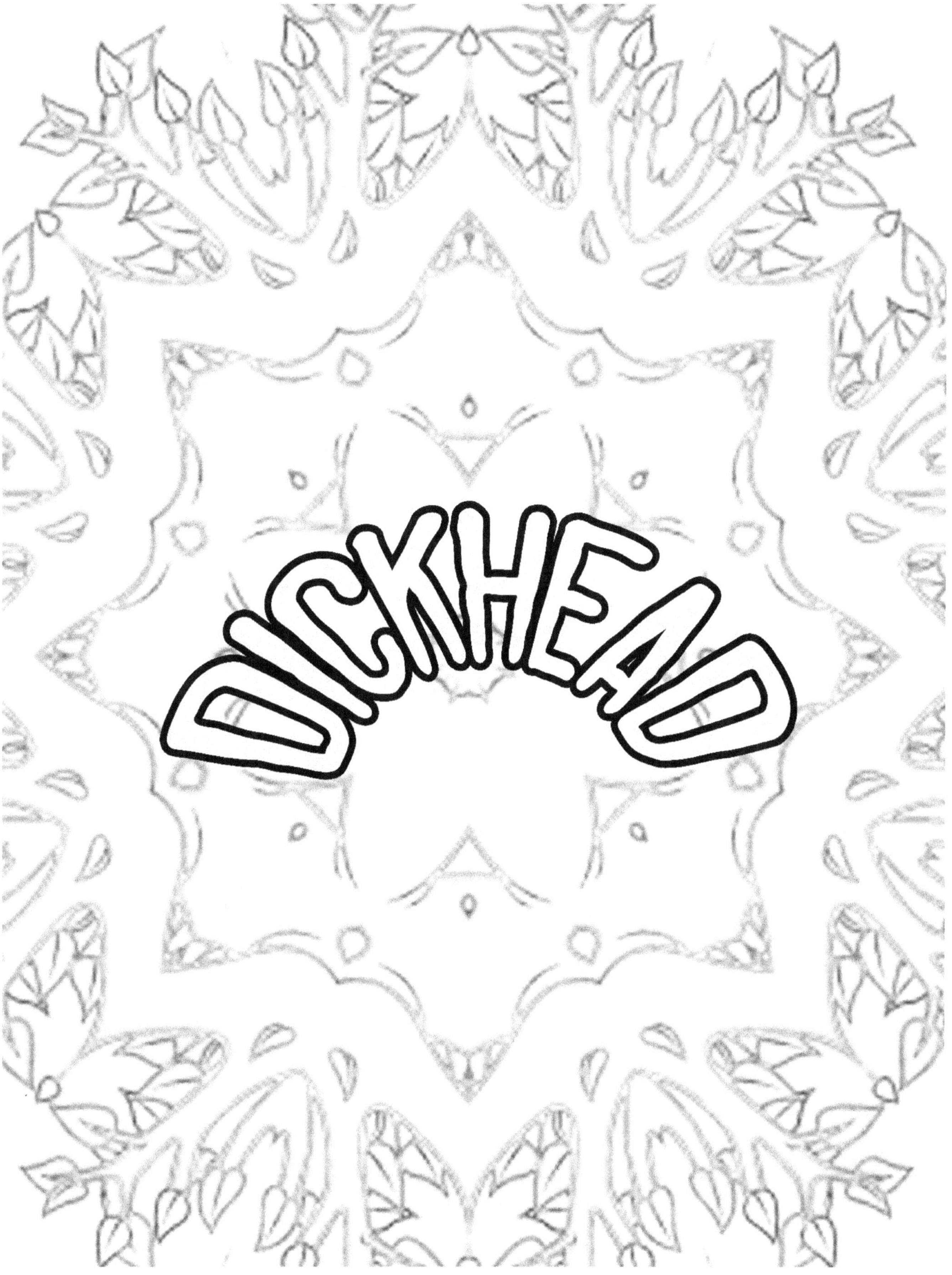
DICKHEAD

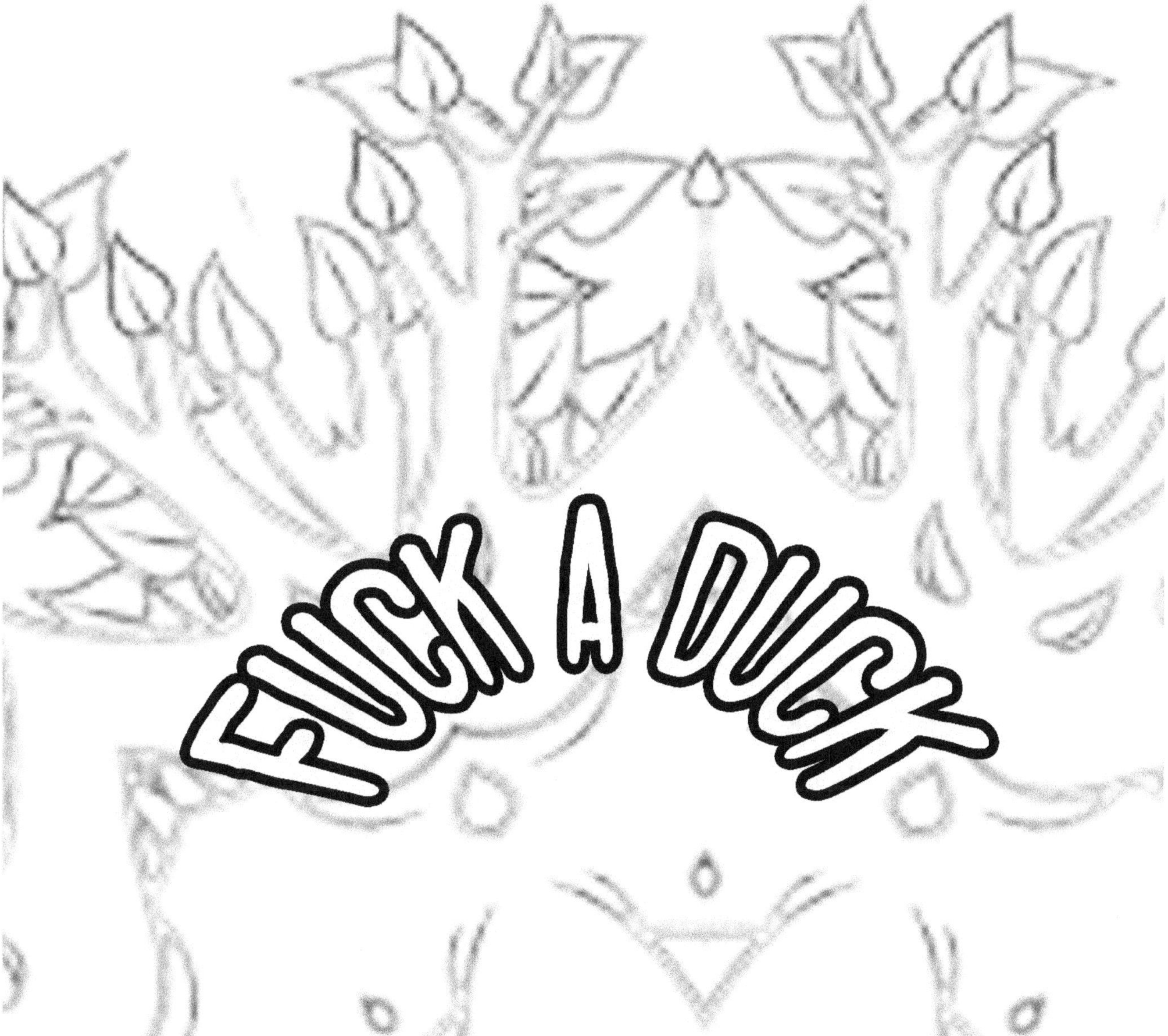
FUCK A DUCK

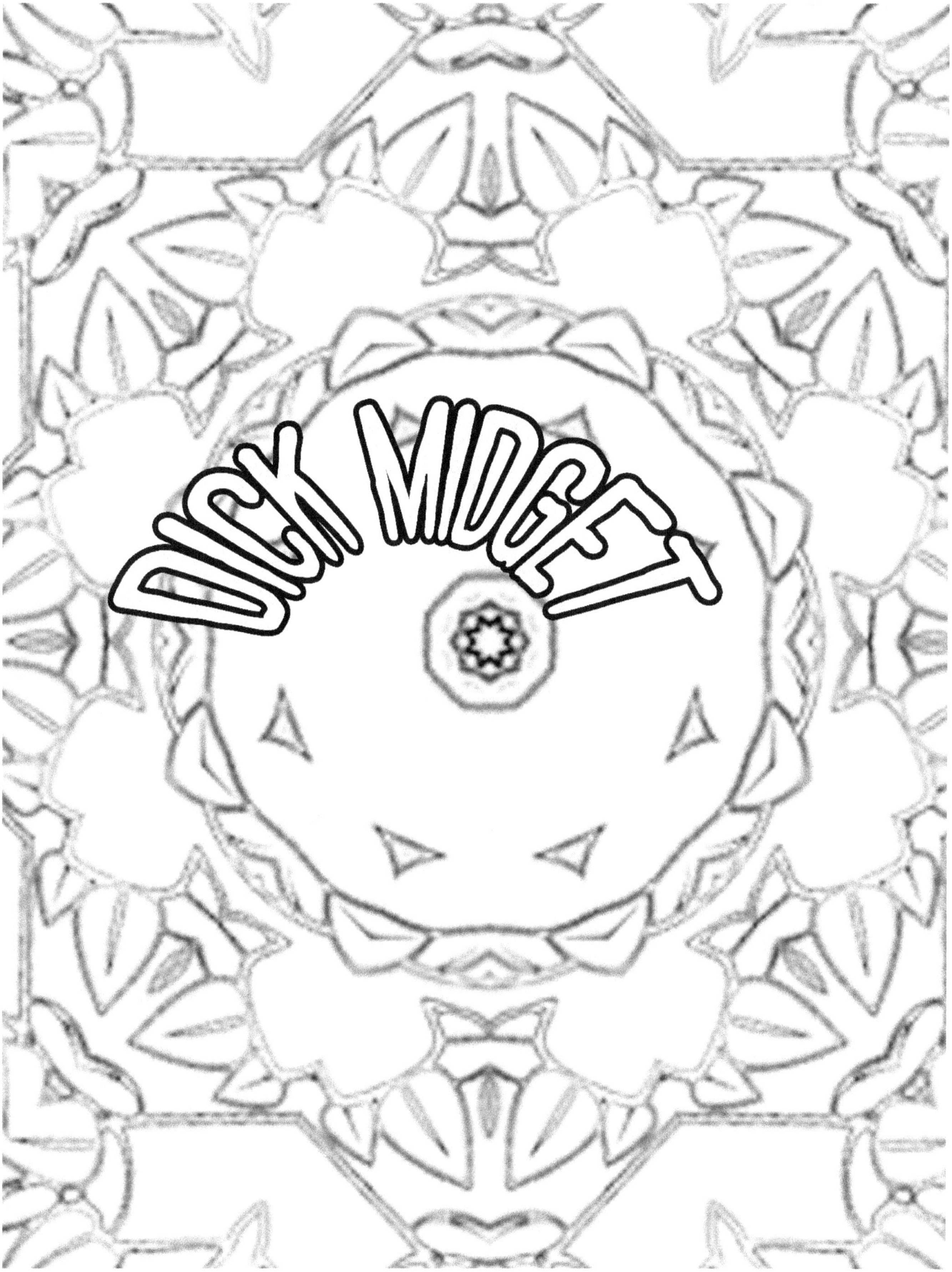
DICK MIDGET

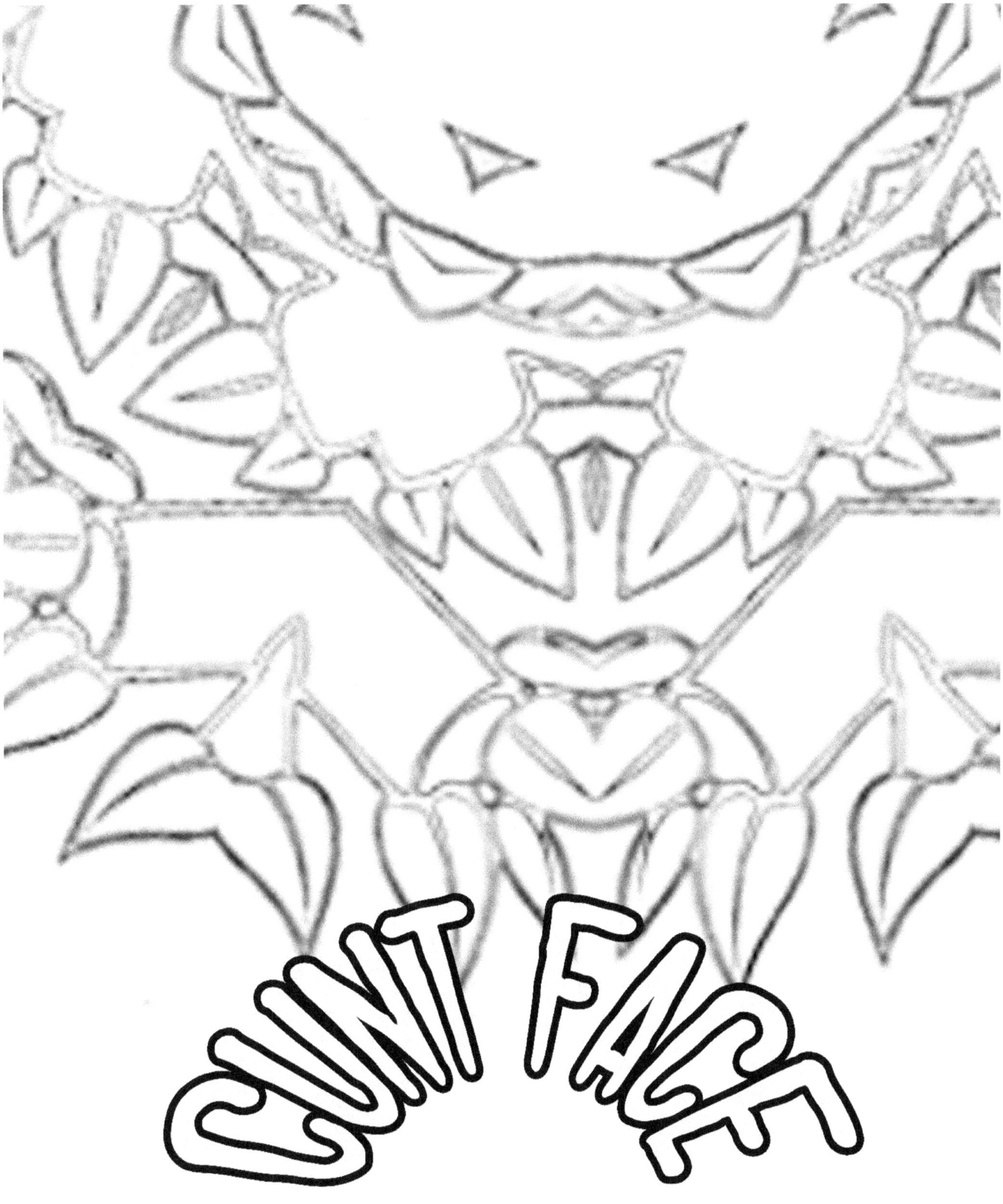
CUNT FACE

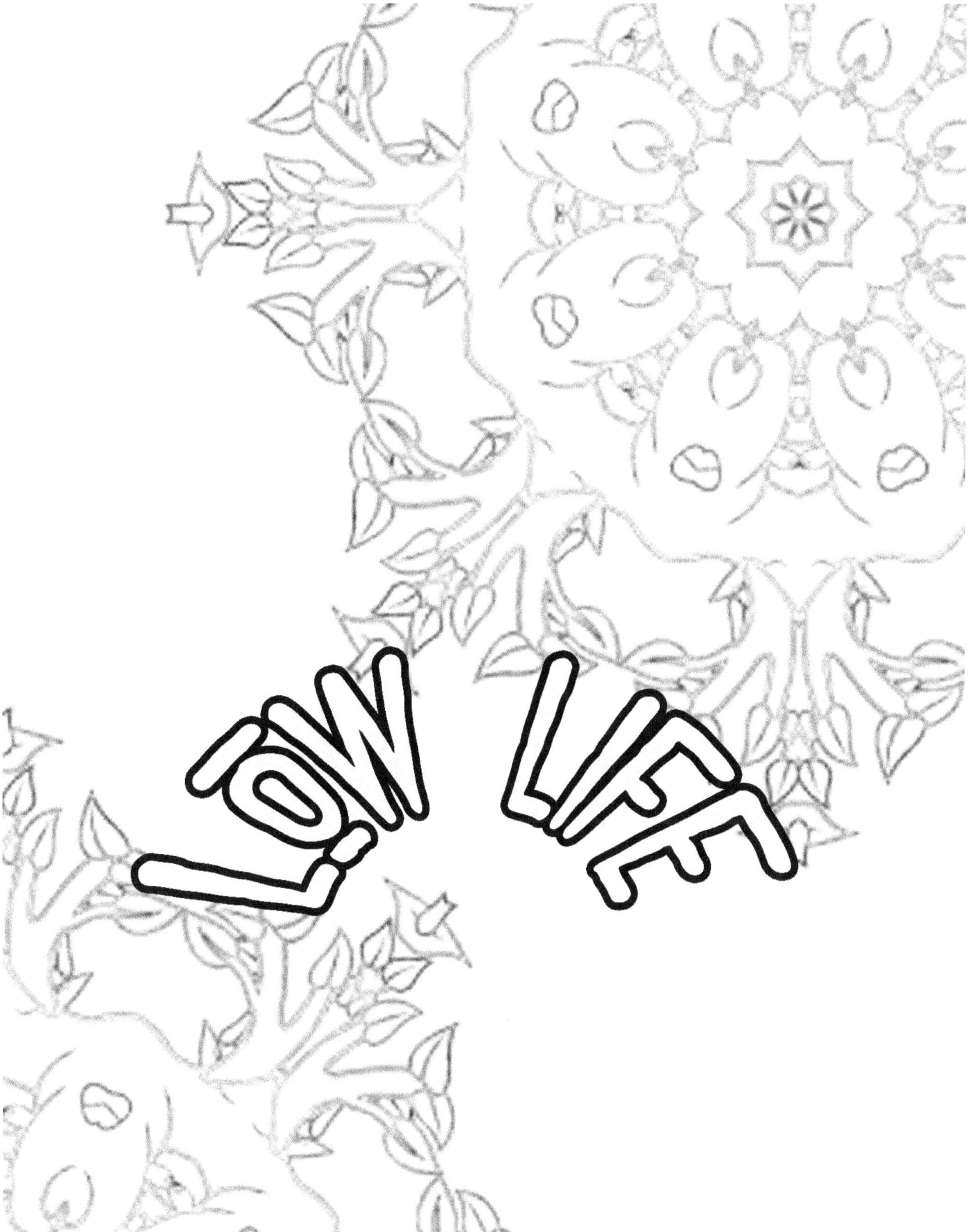
LOW LIFE

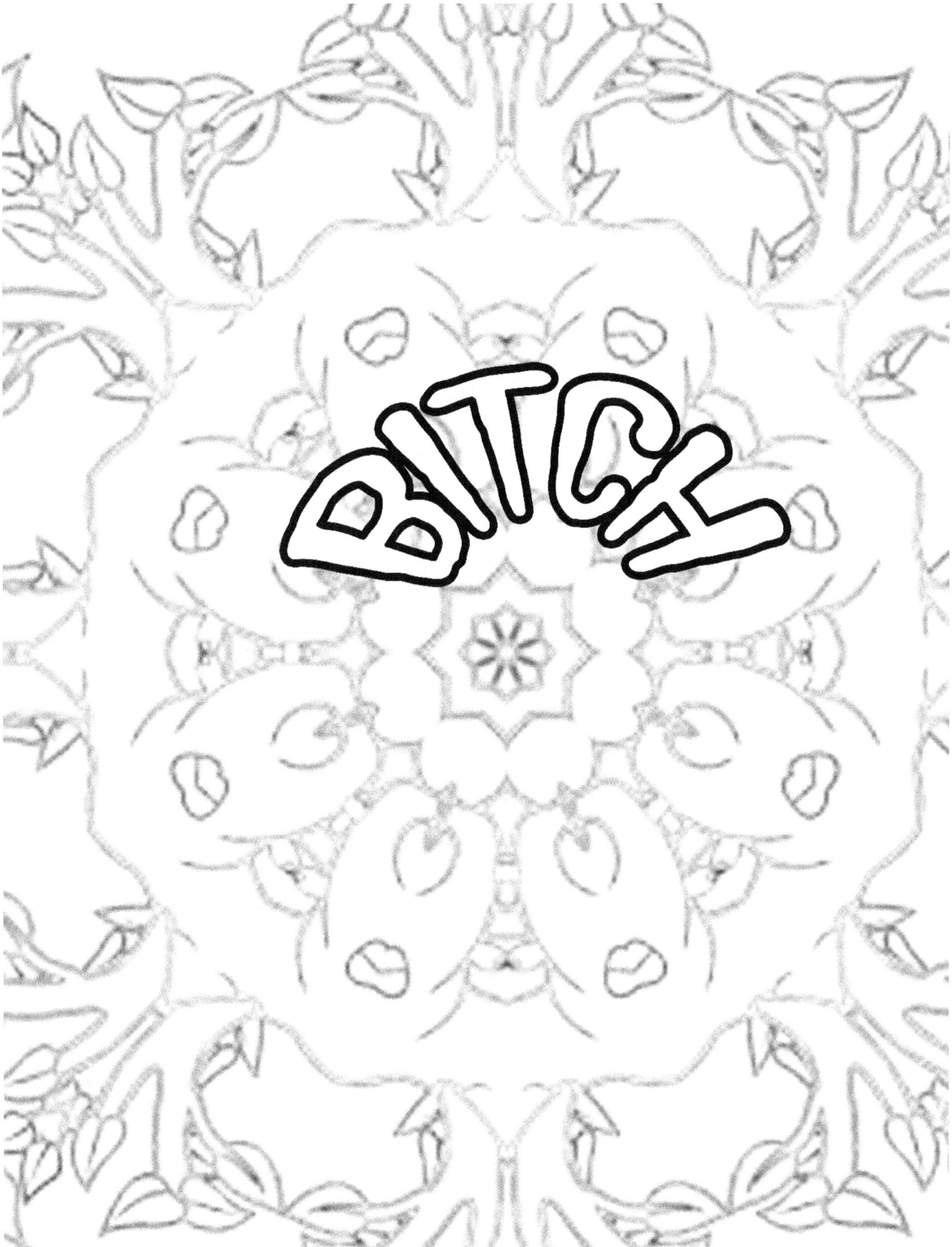
BITCH

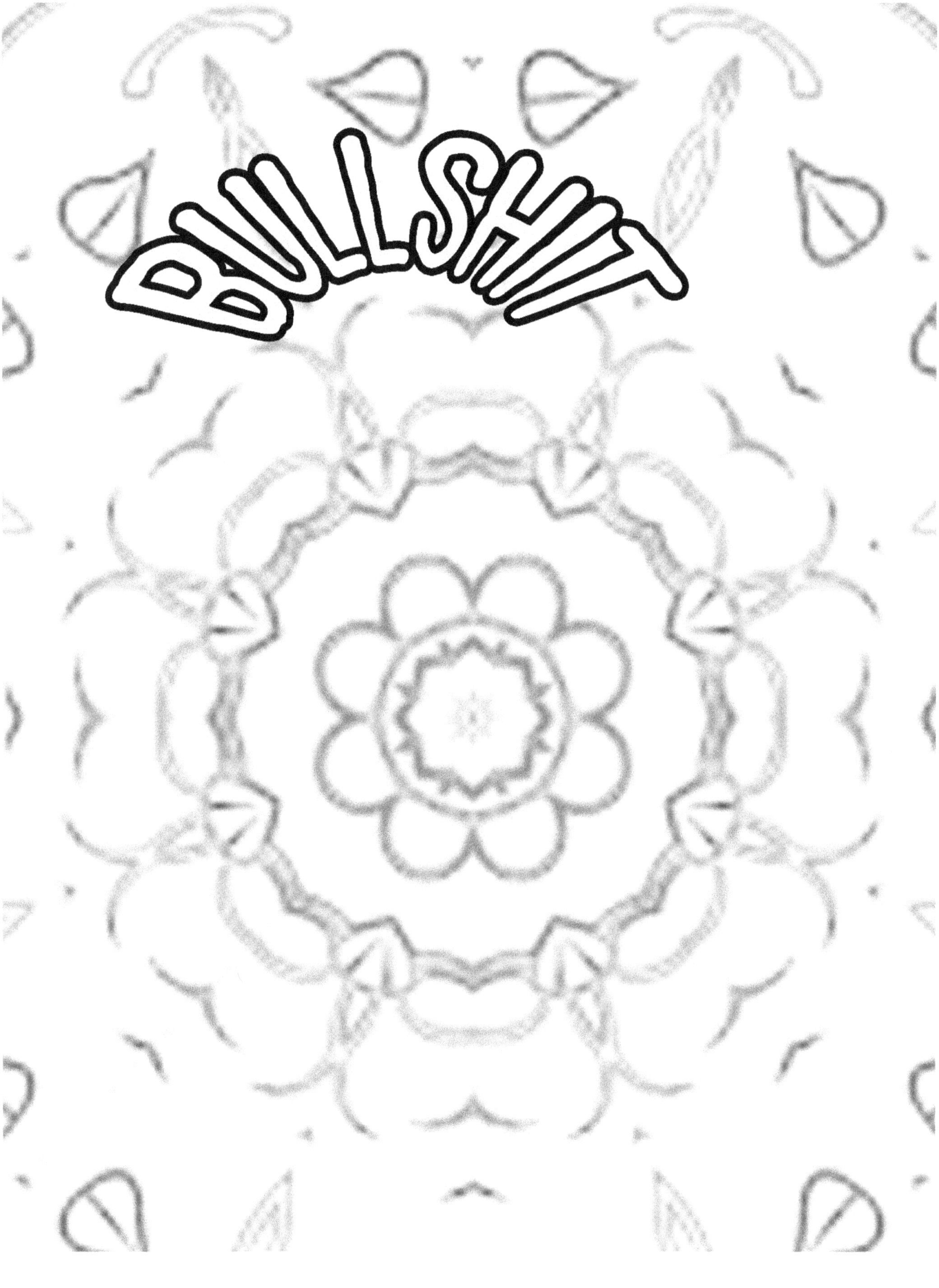
BULLSHIT

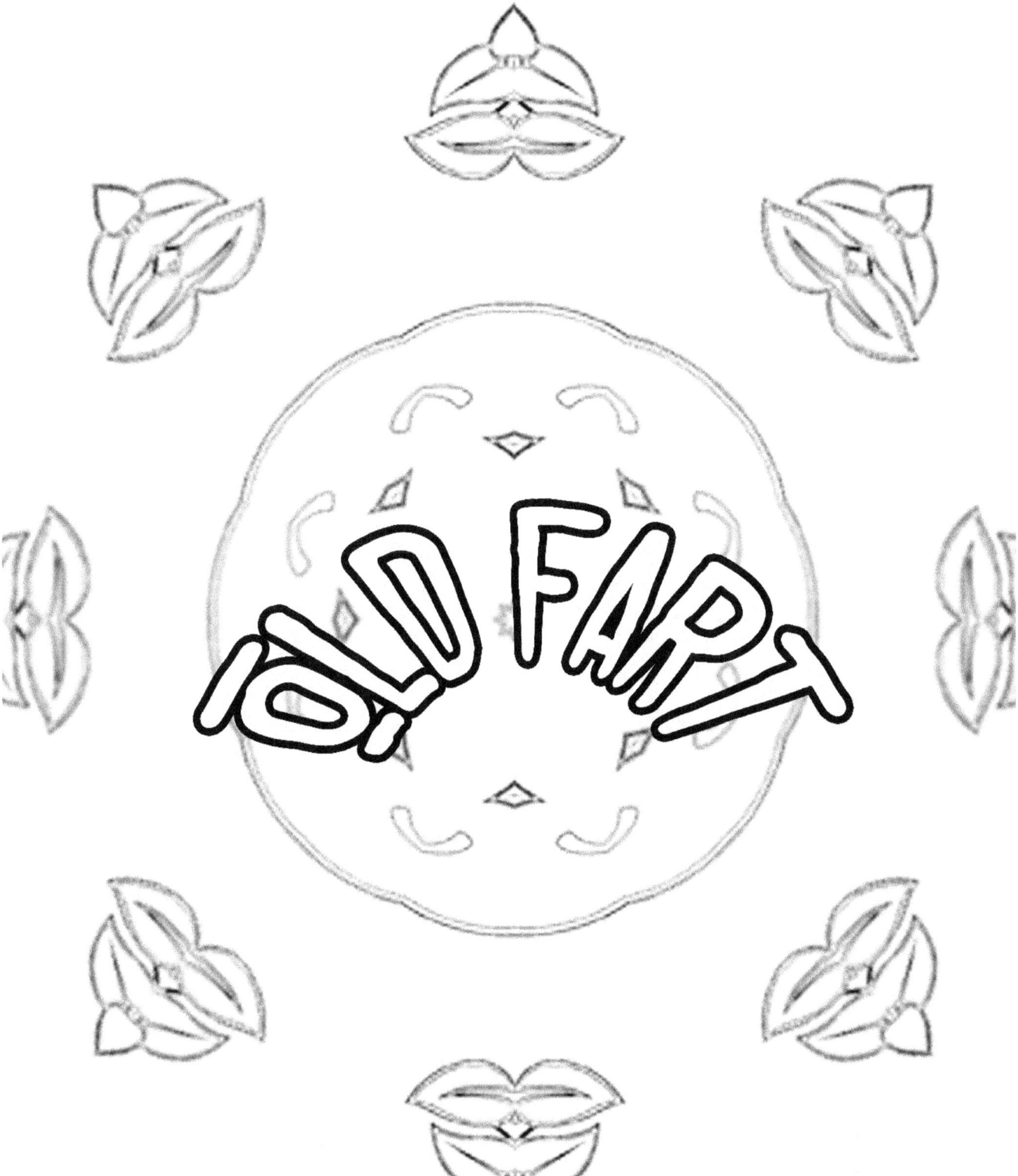
OLD FART

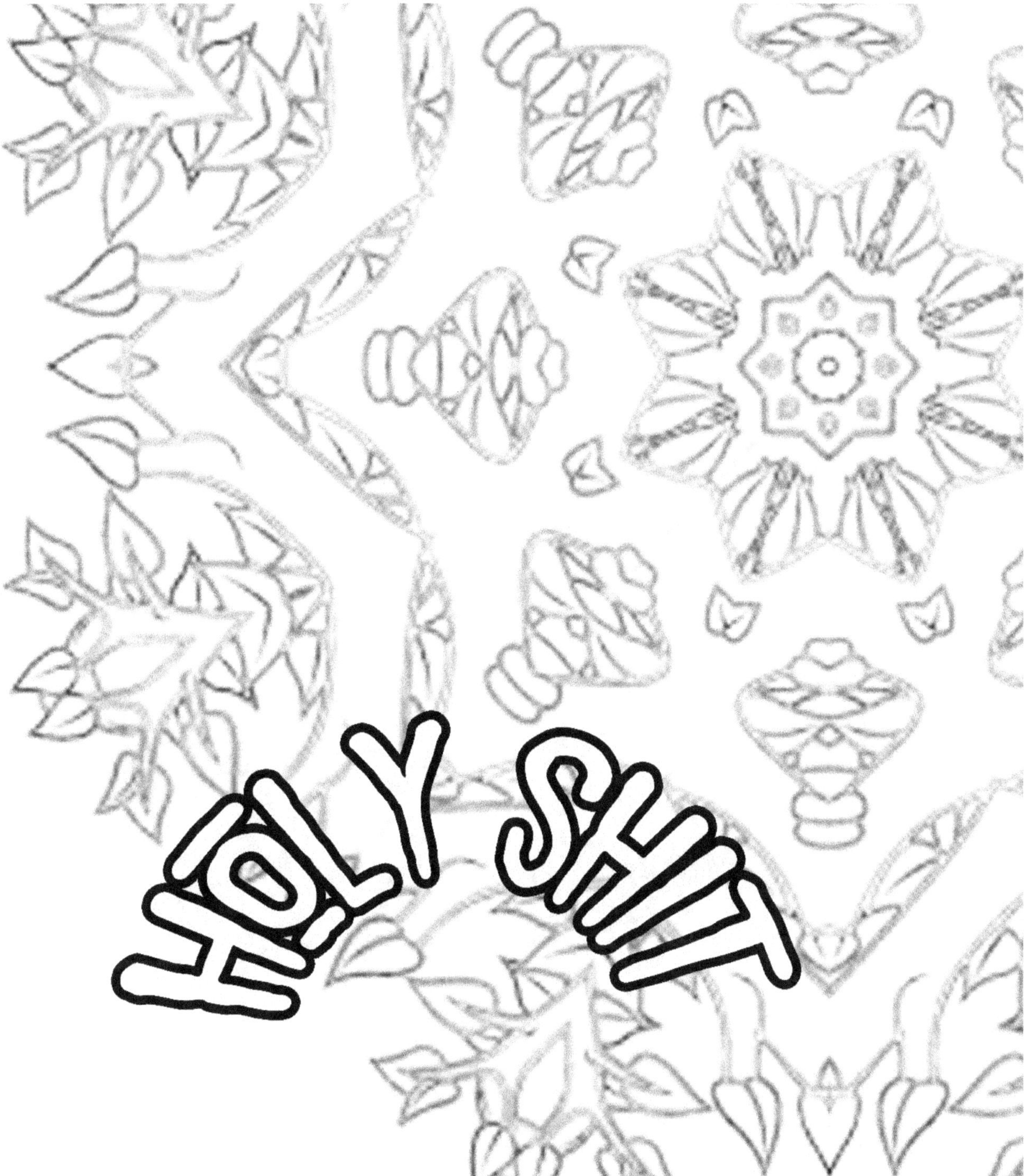
HOLY SHIT

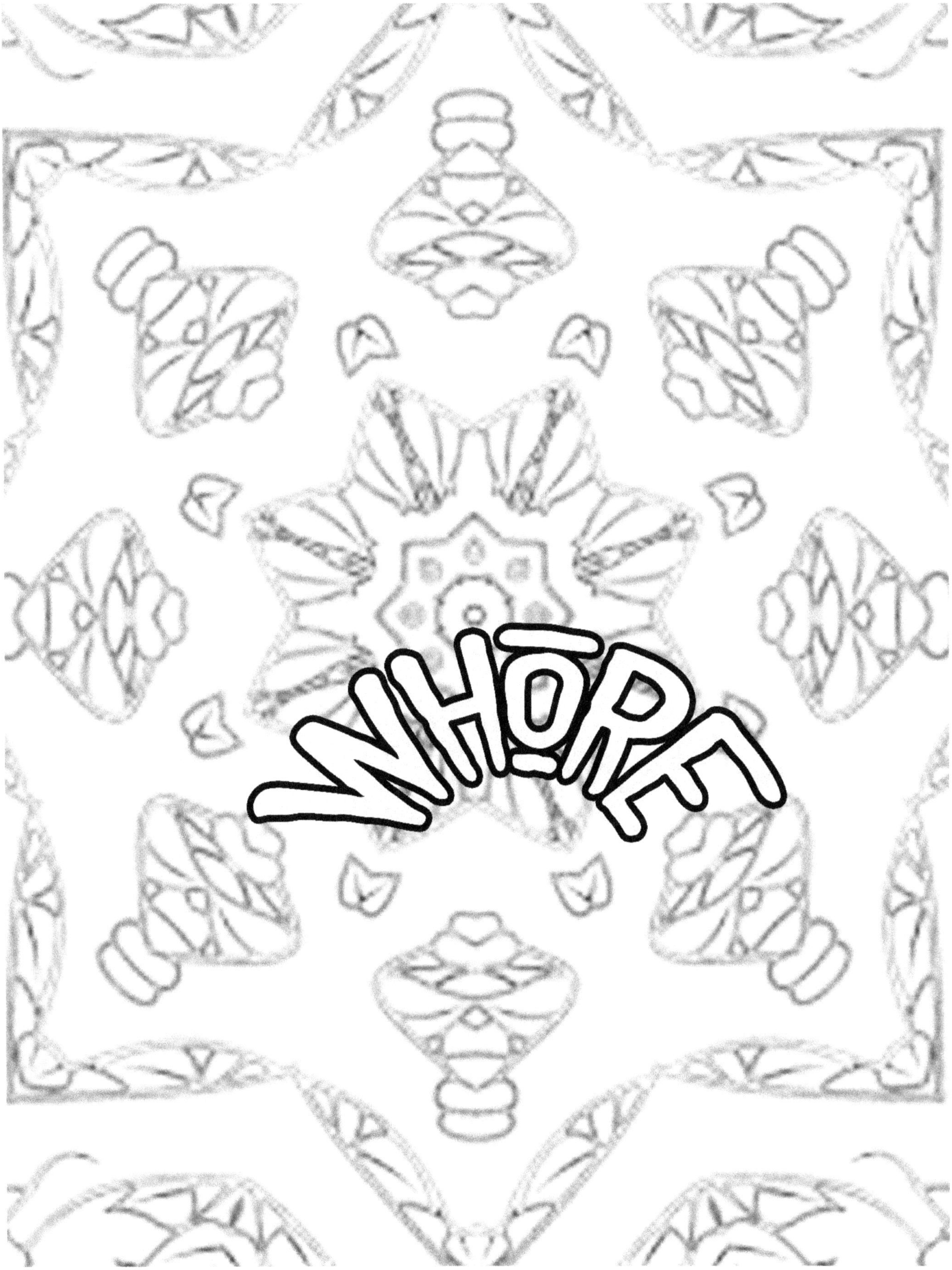
WHORE

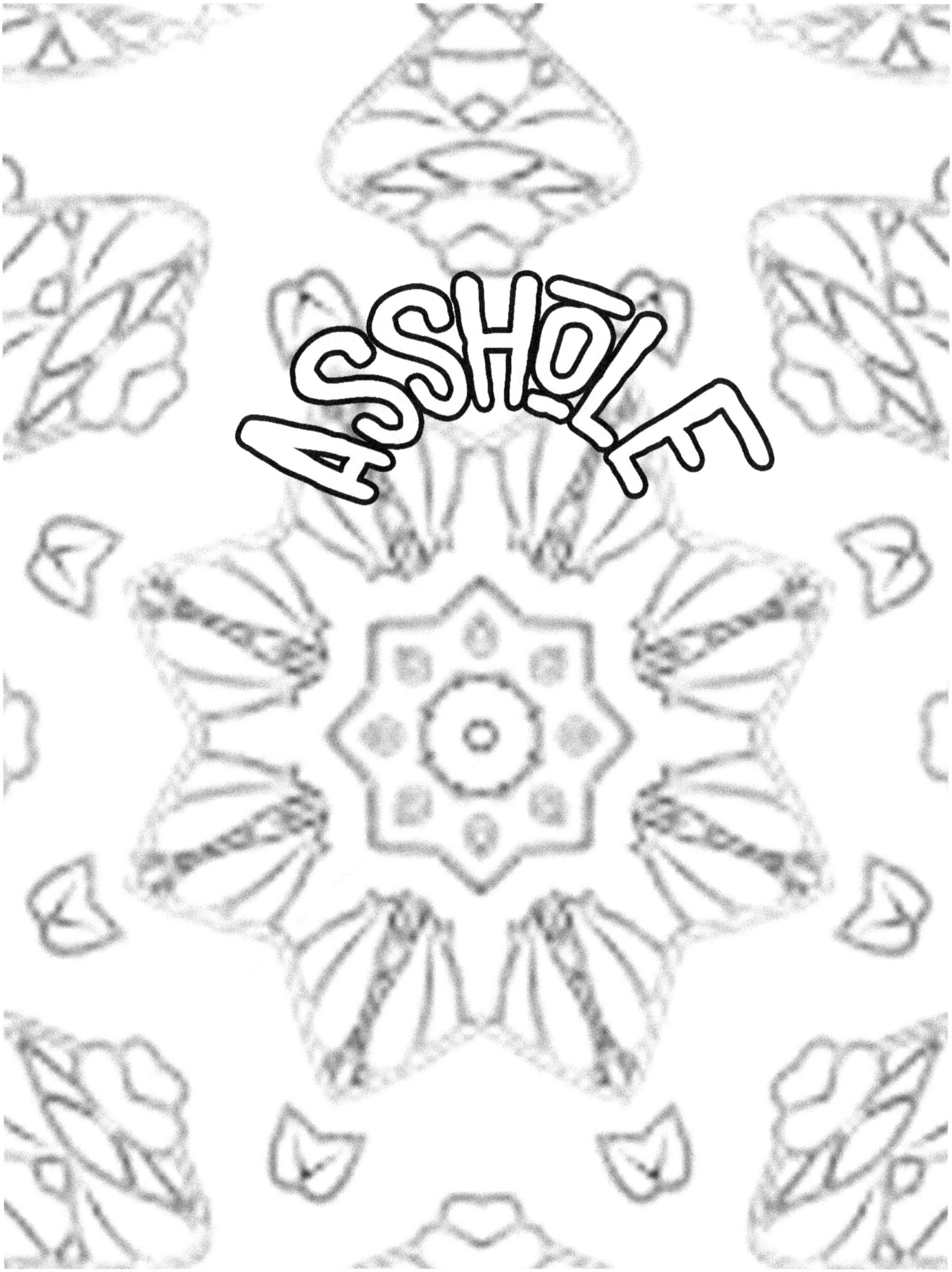
ASSHOLE

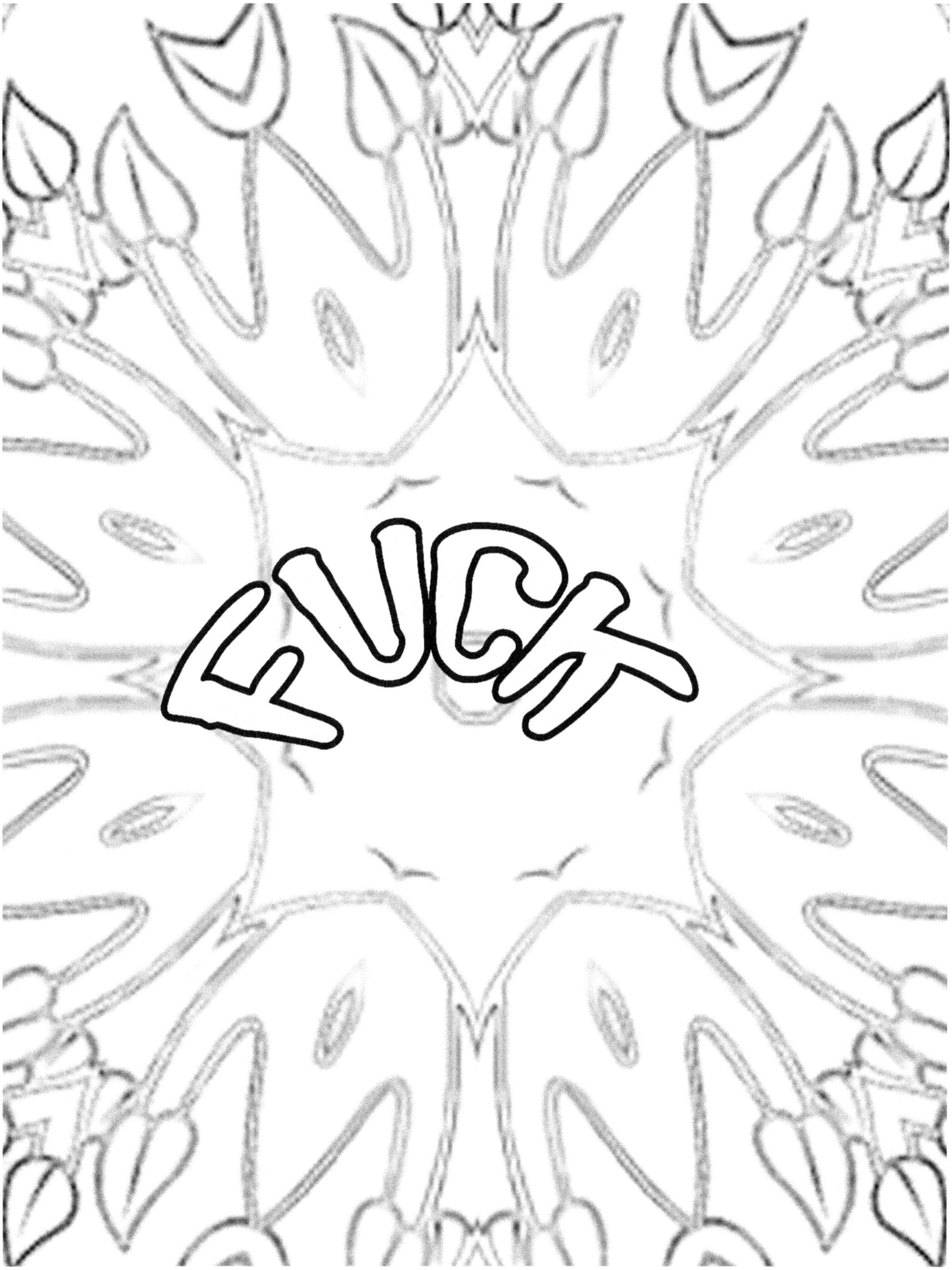
FUCK

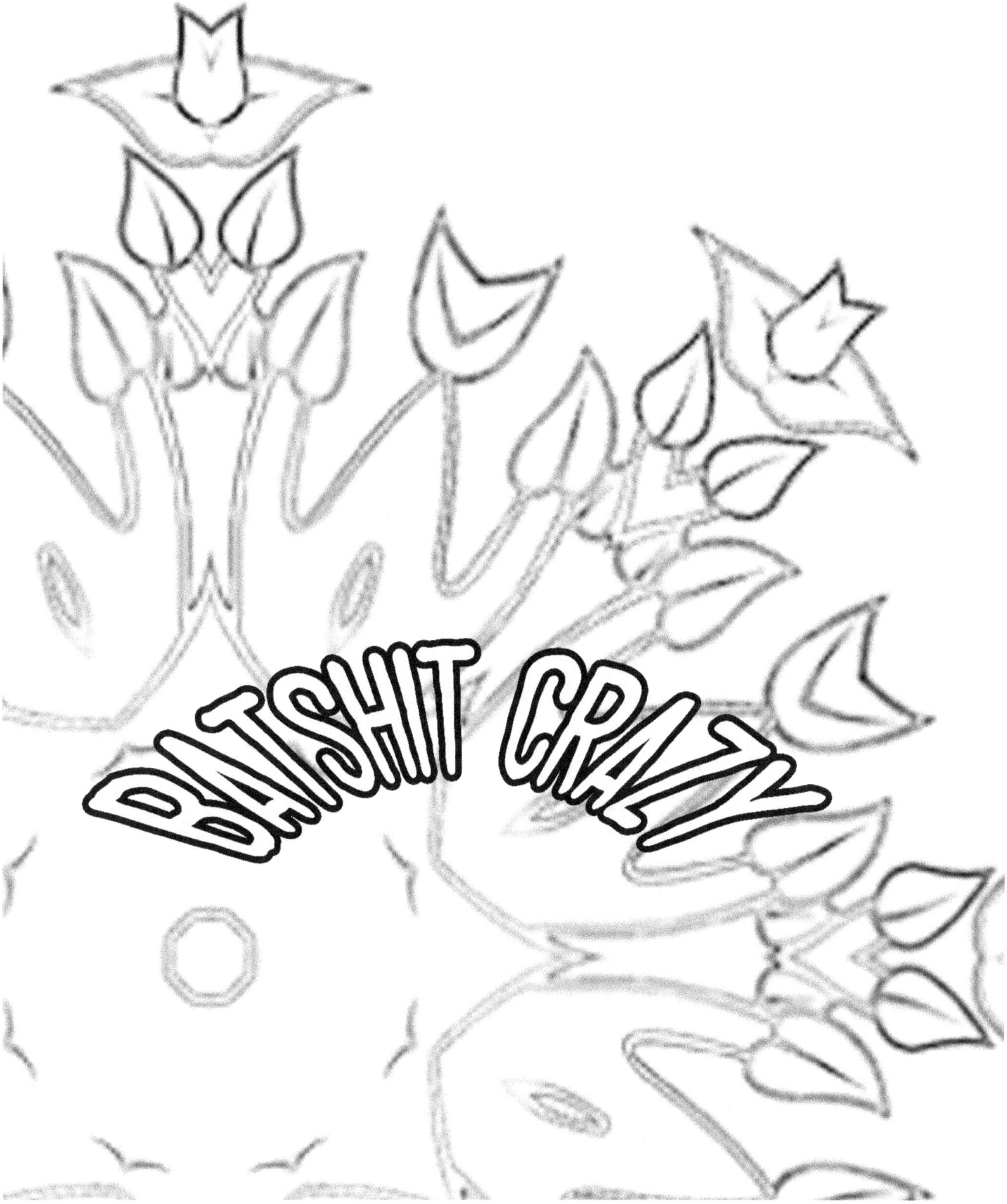
BATSHIT CRAZY

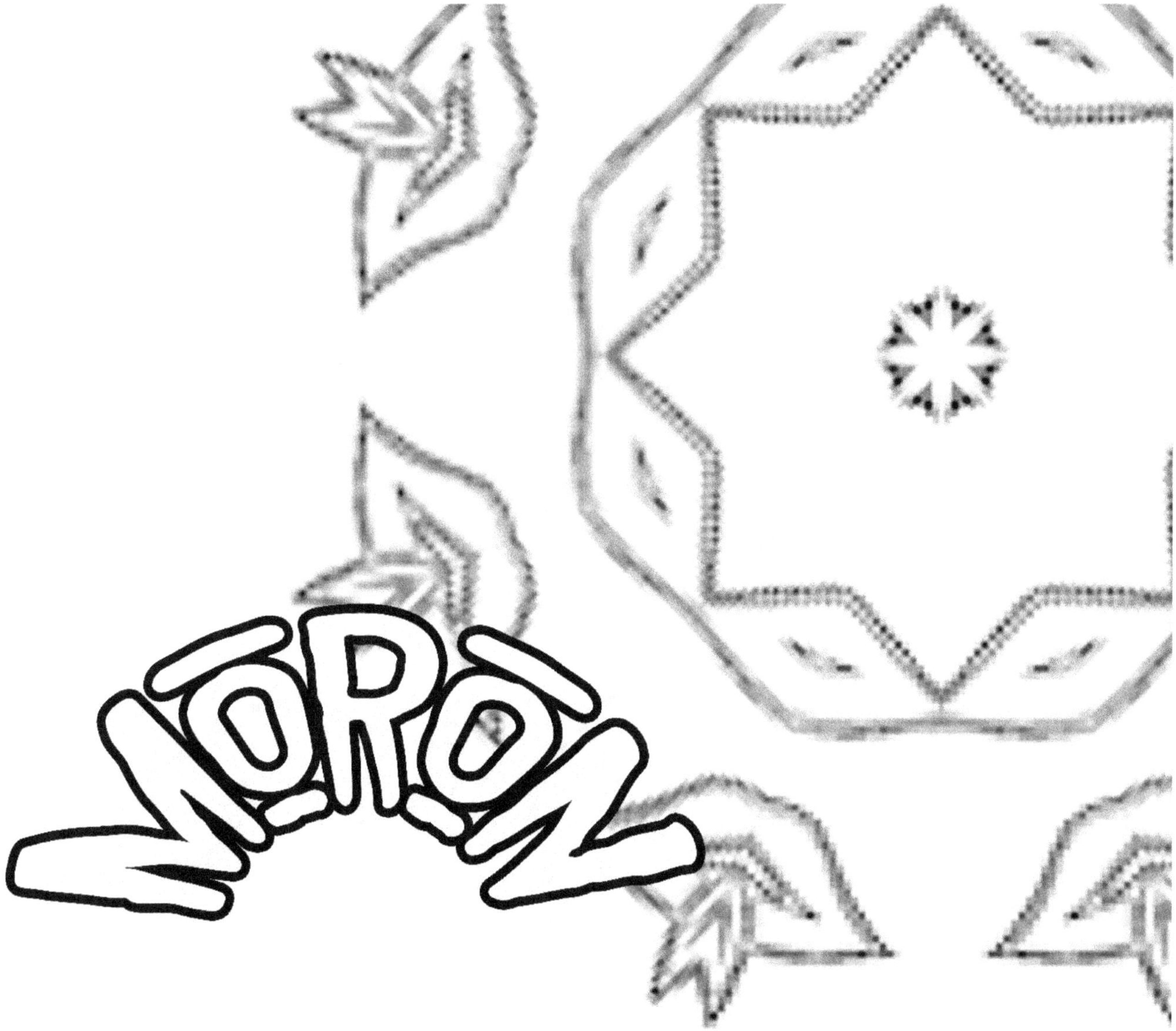
MORON

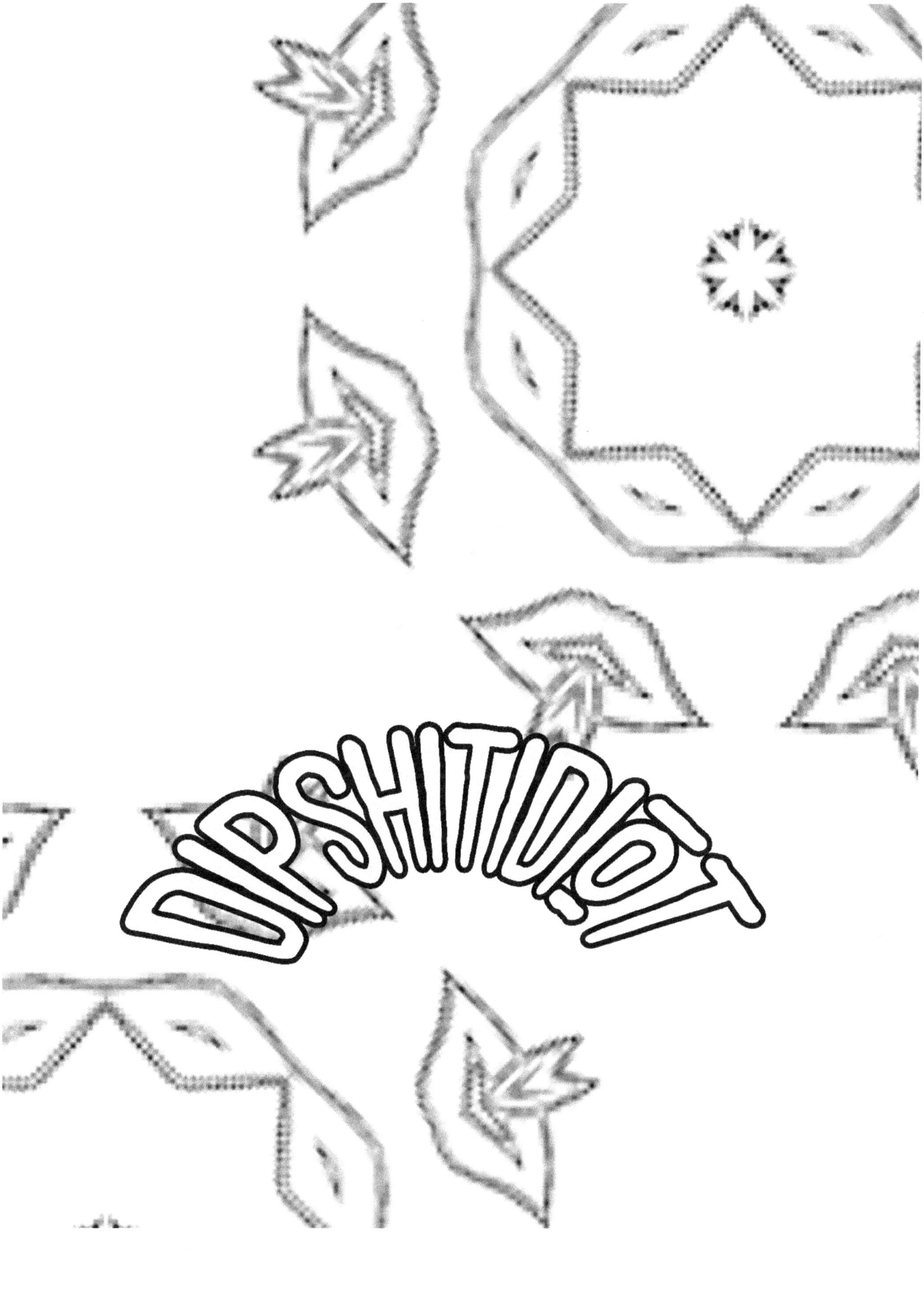
DIPSHITIDIOT

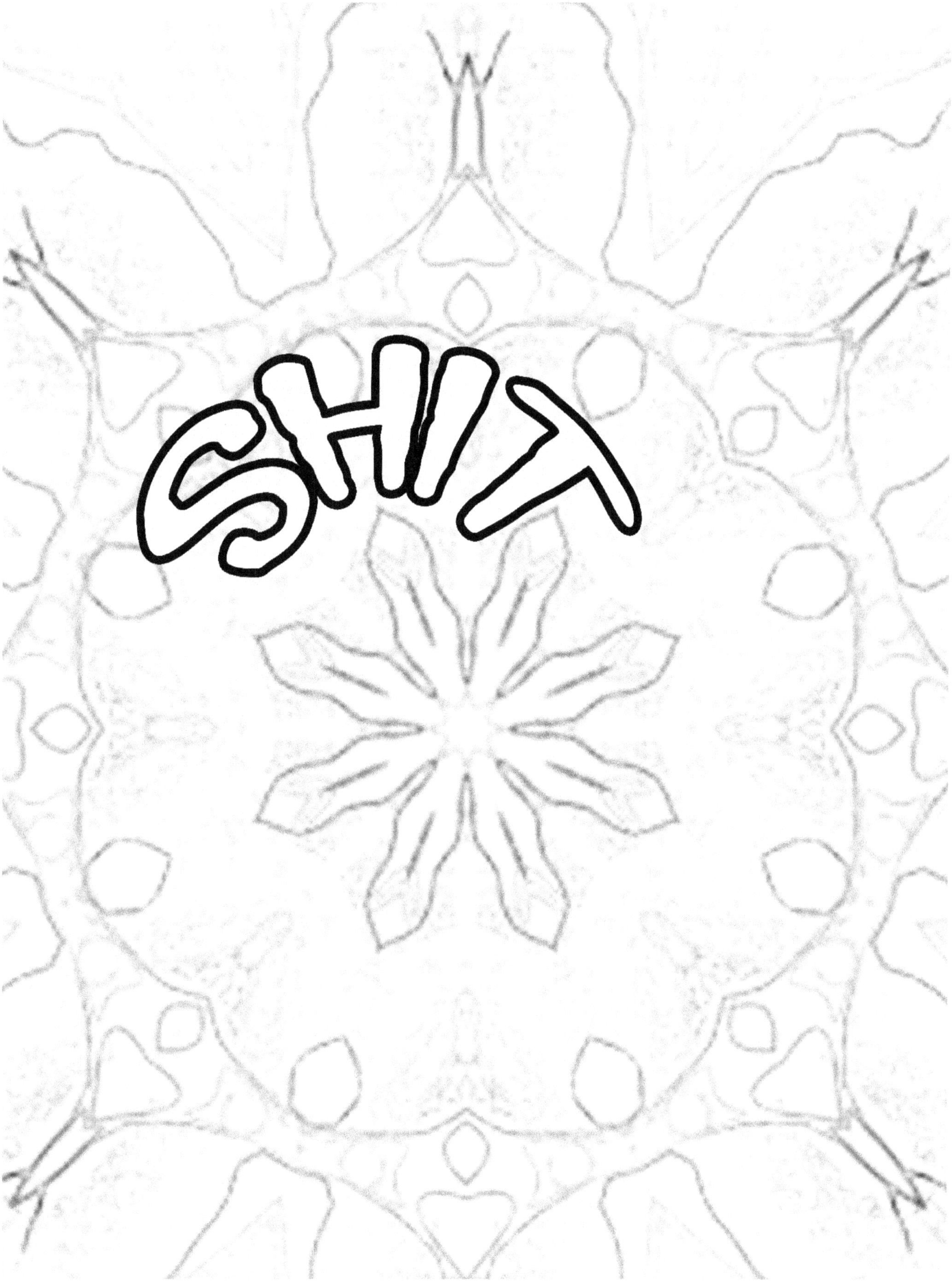
SHIT

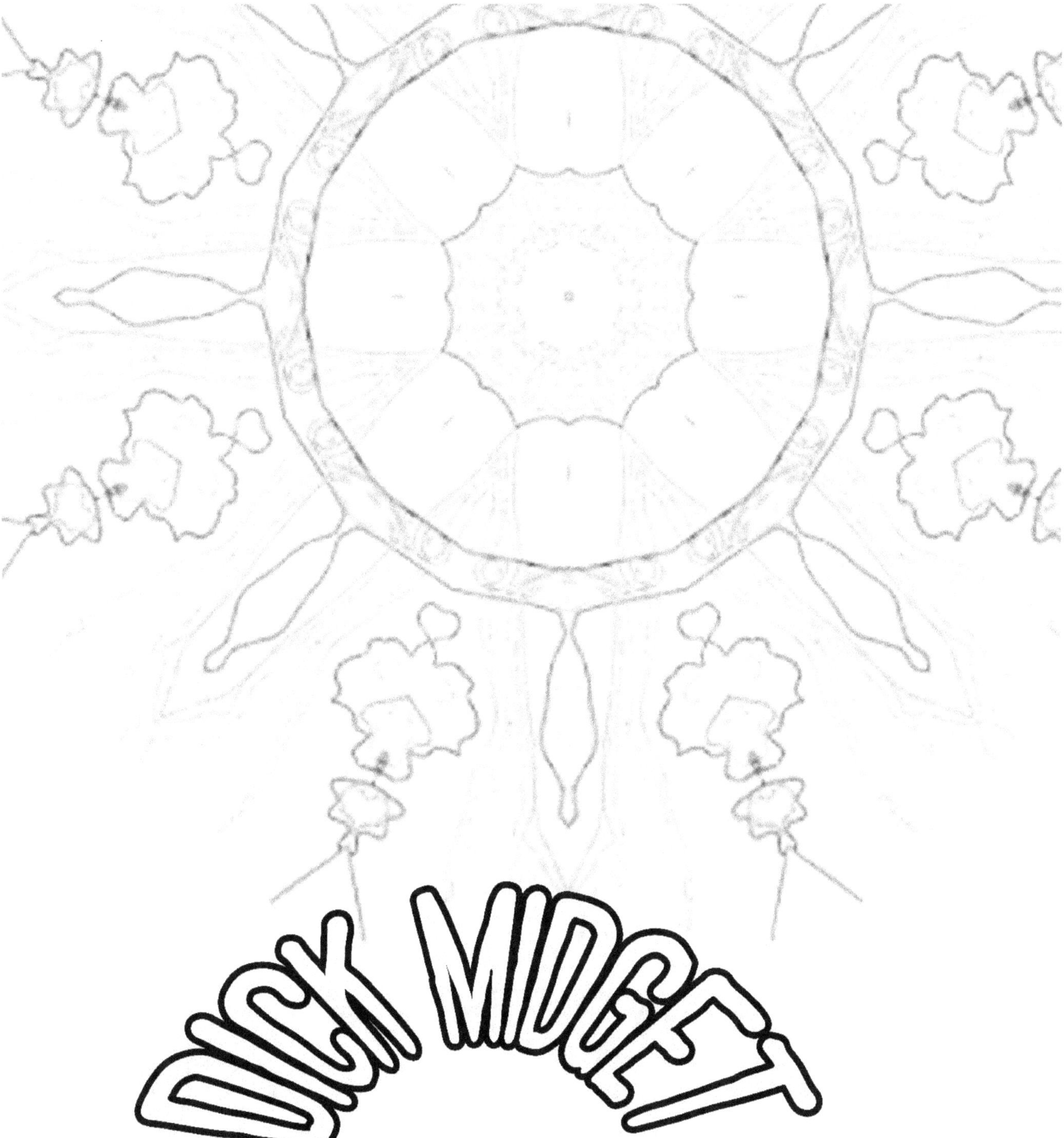

DICK MIDGET

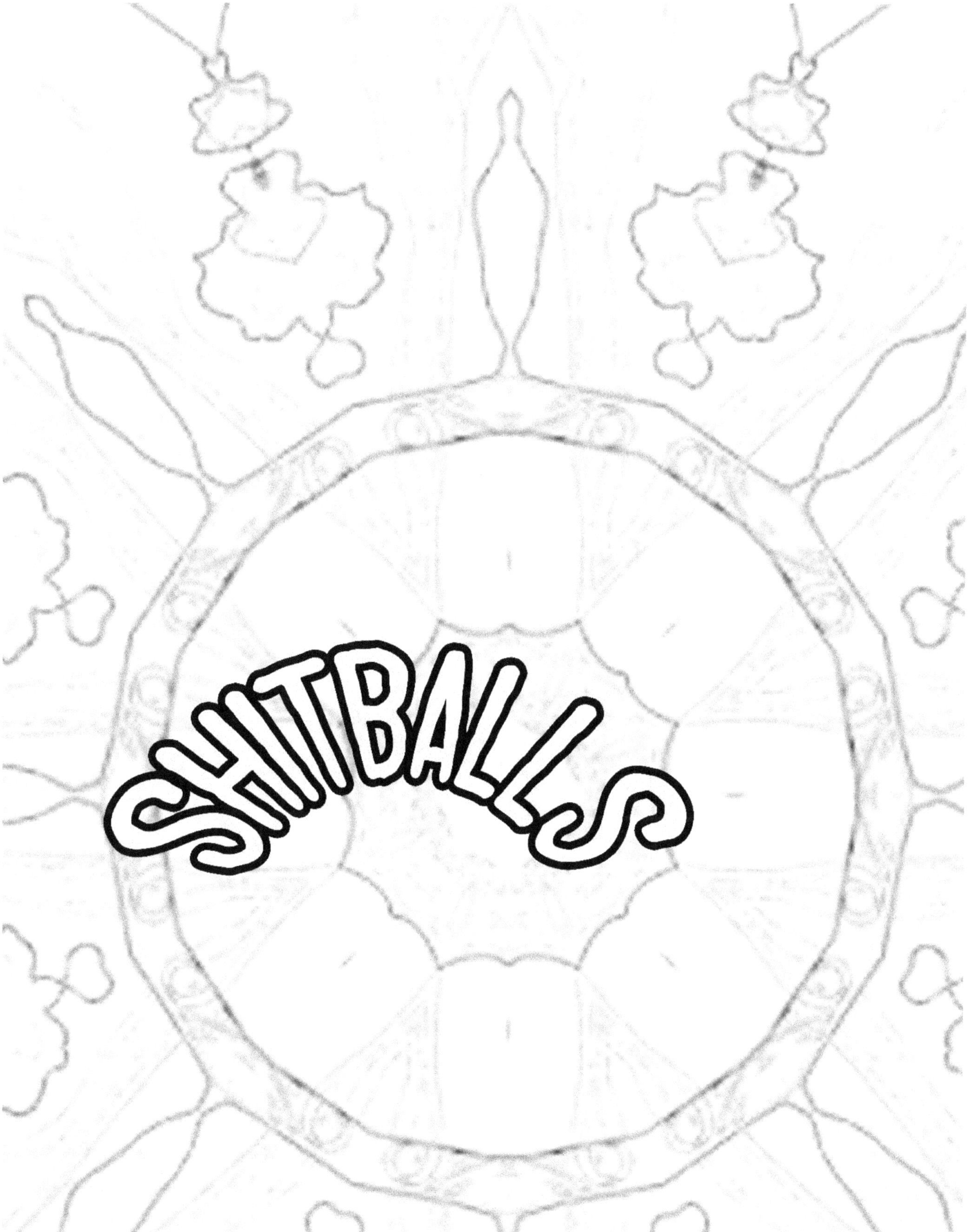
SHITBALLS

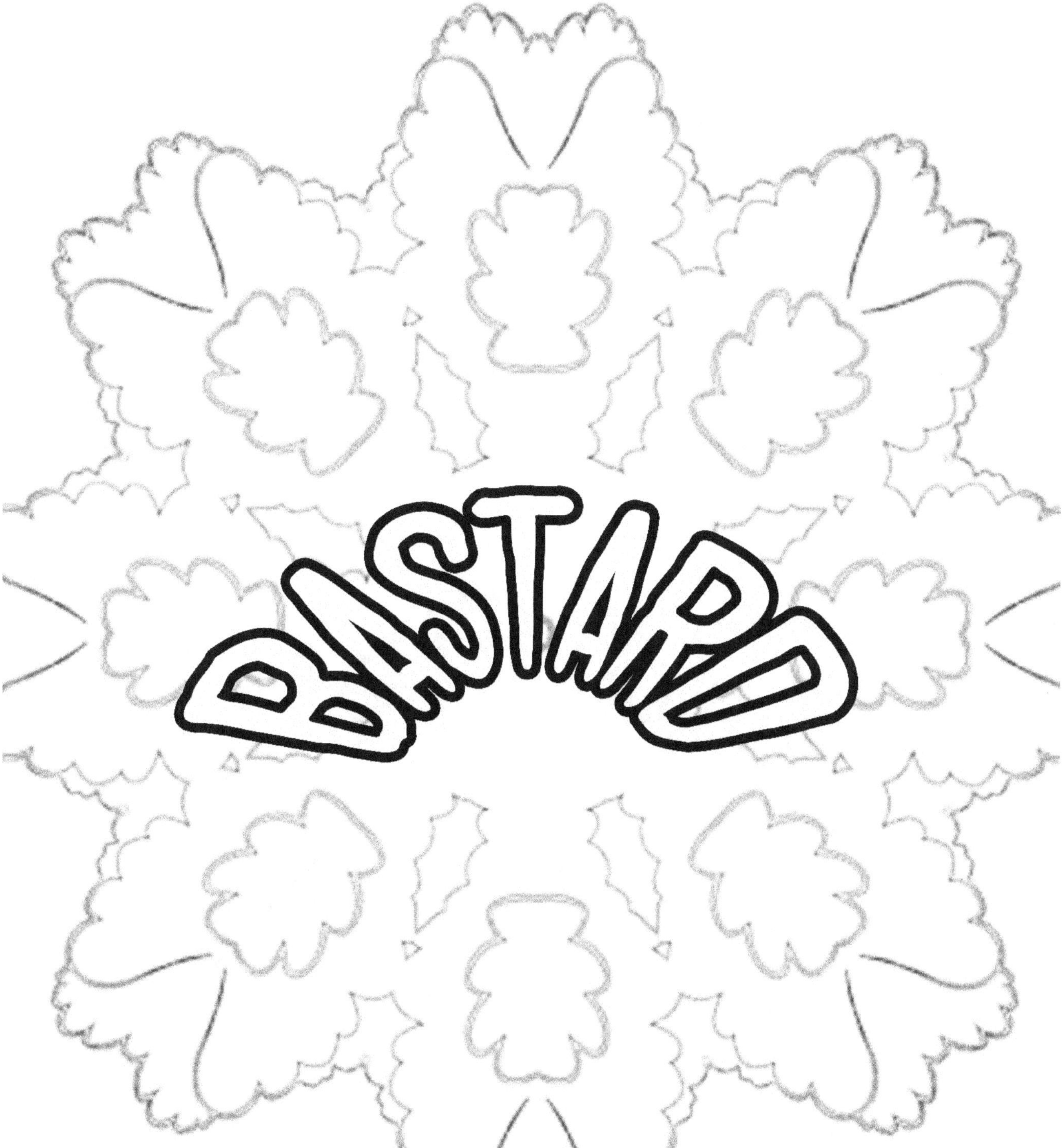
BASTARD

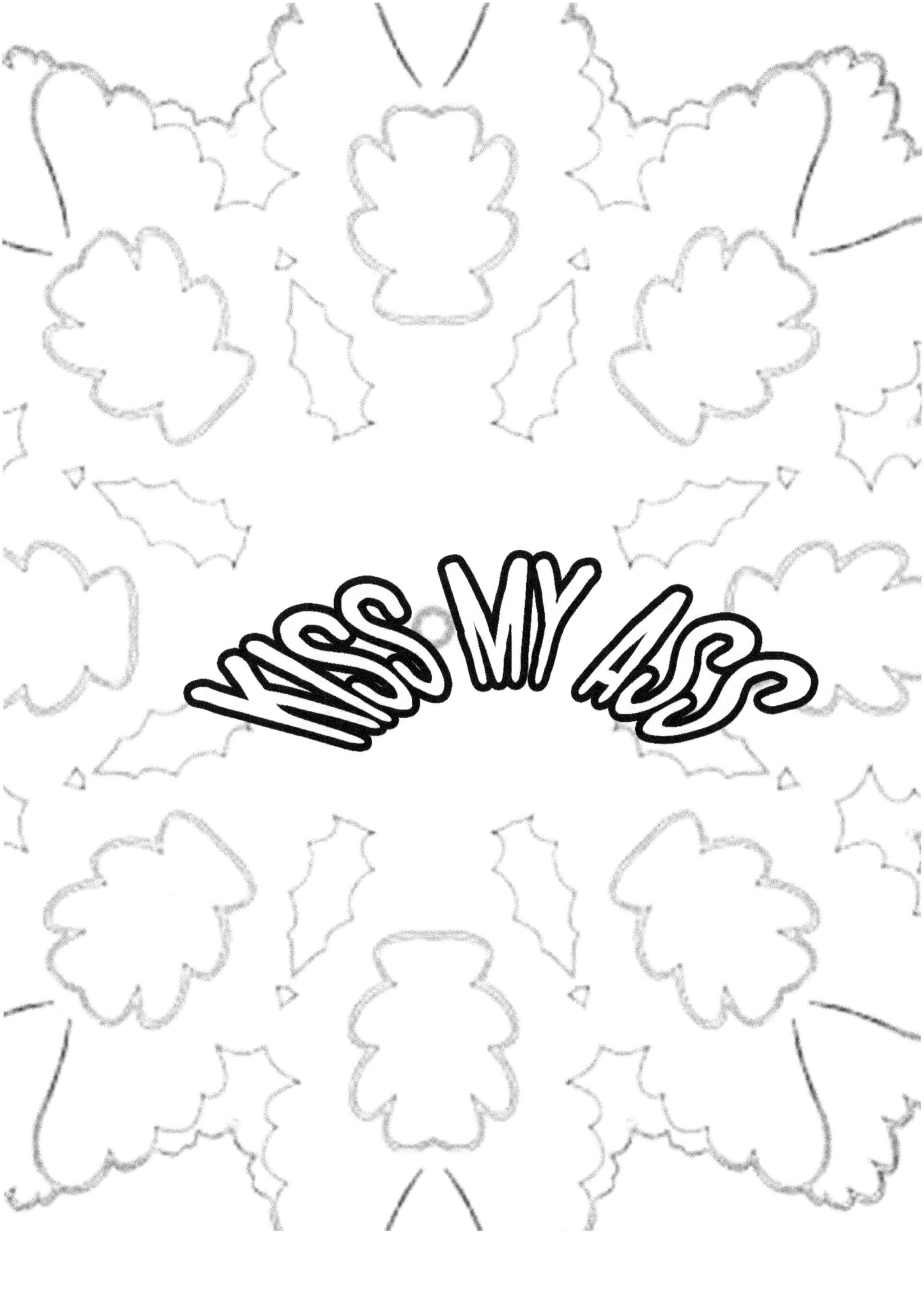
KISS MY ASS

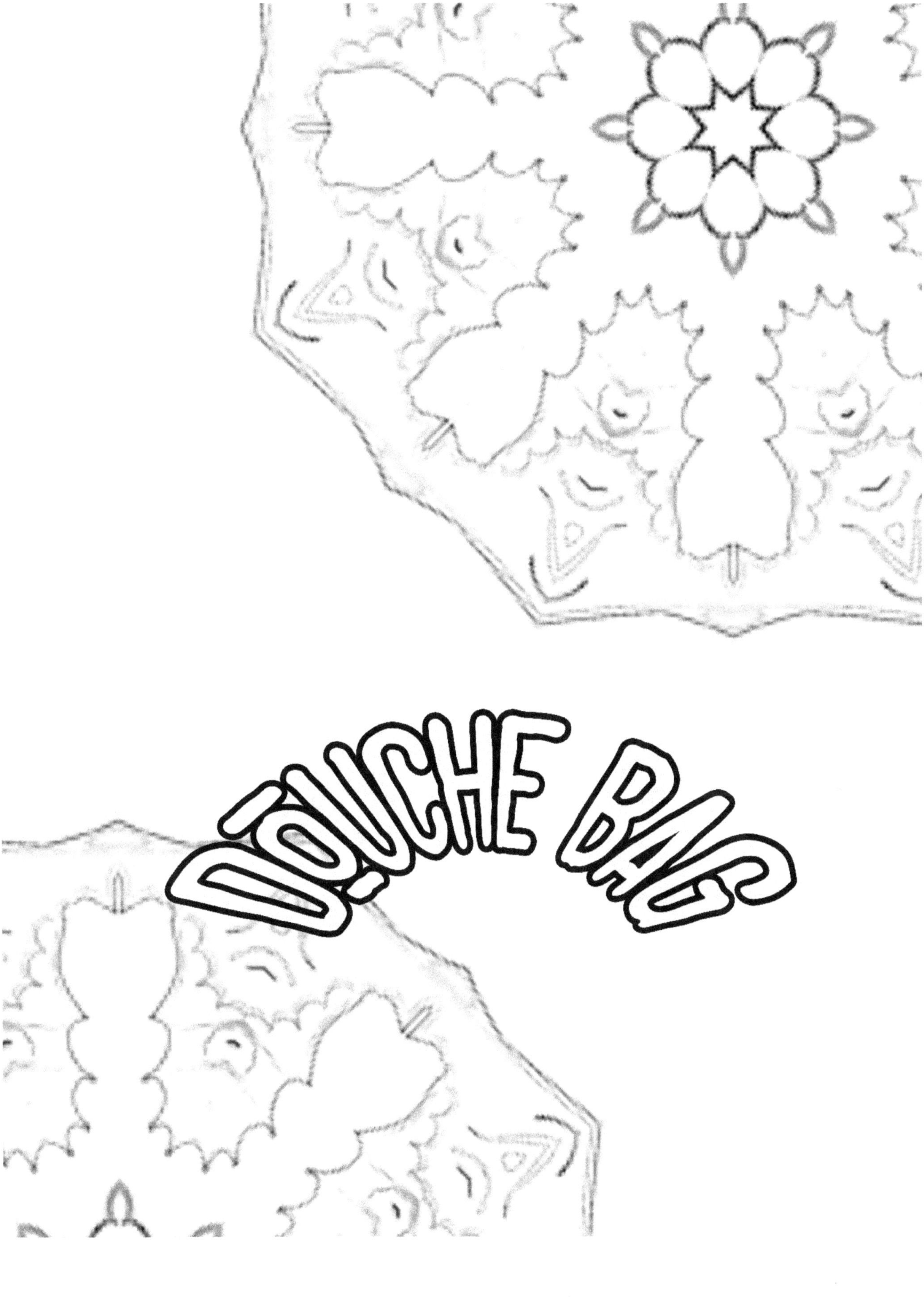
DOUCHE BAG

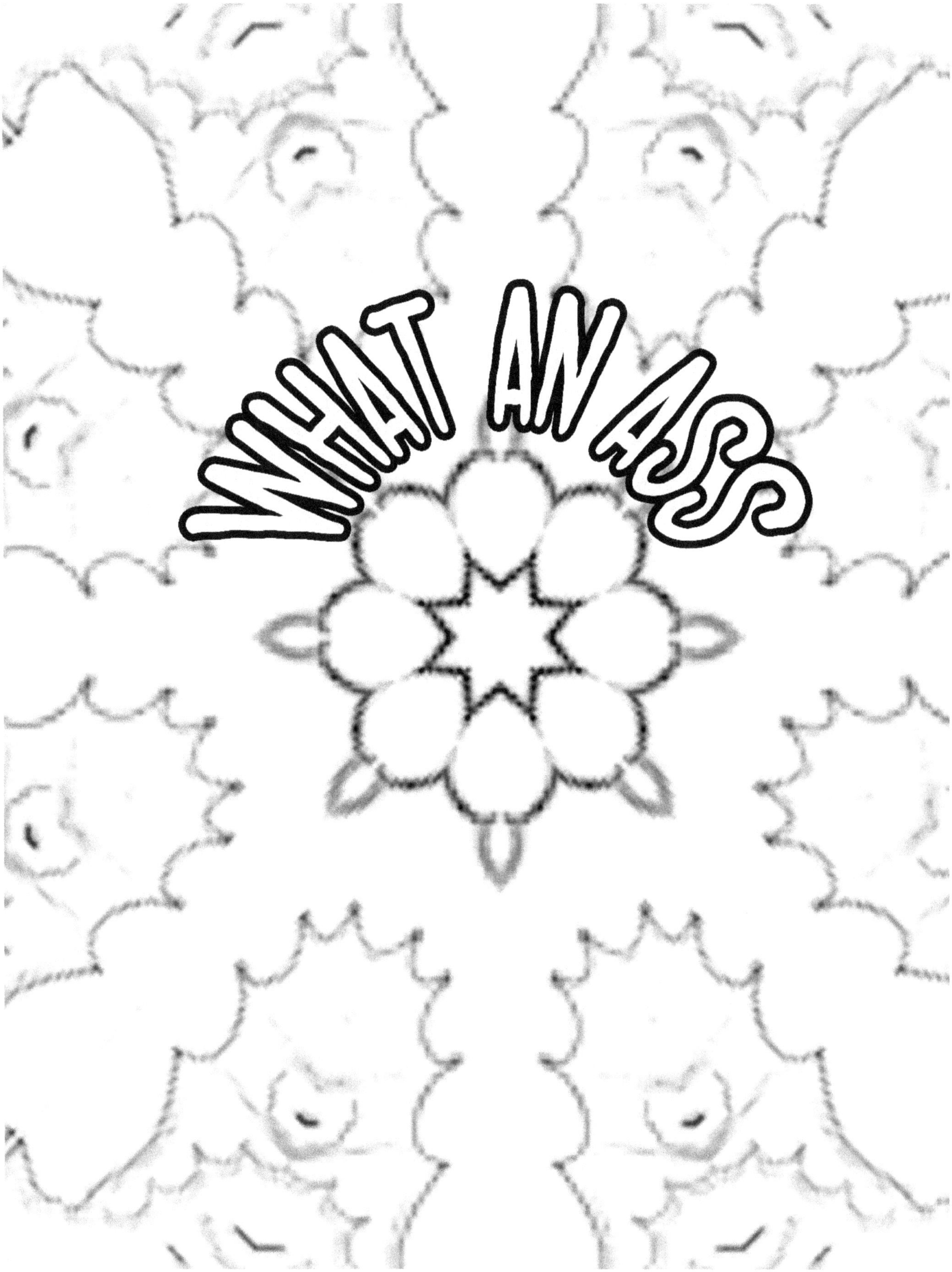
WHAT AN ASS

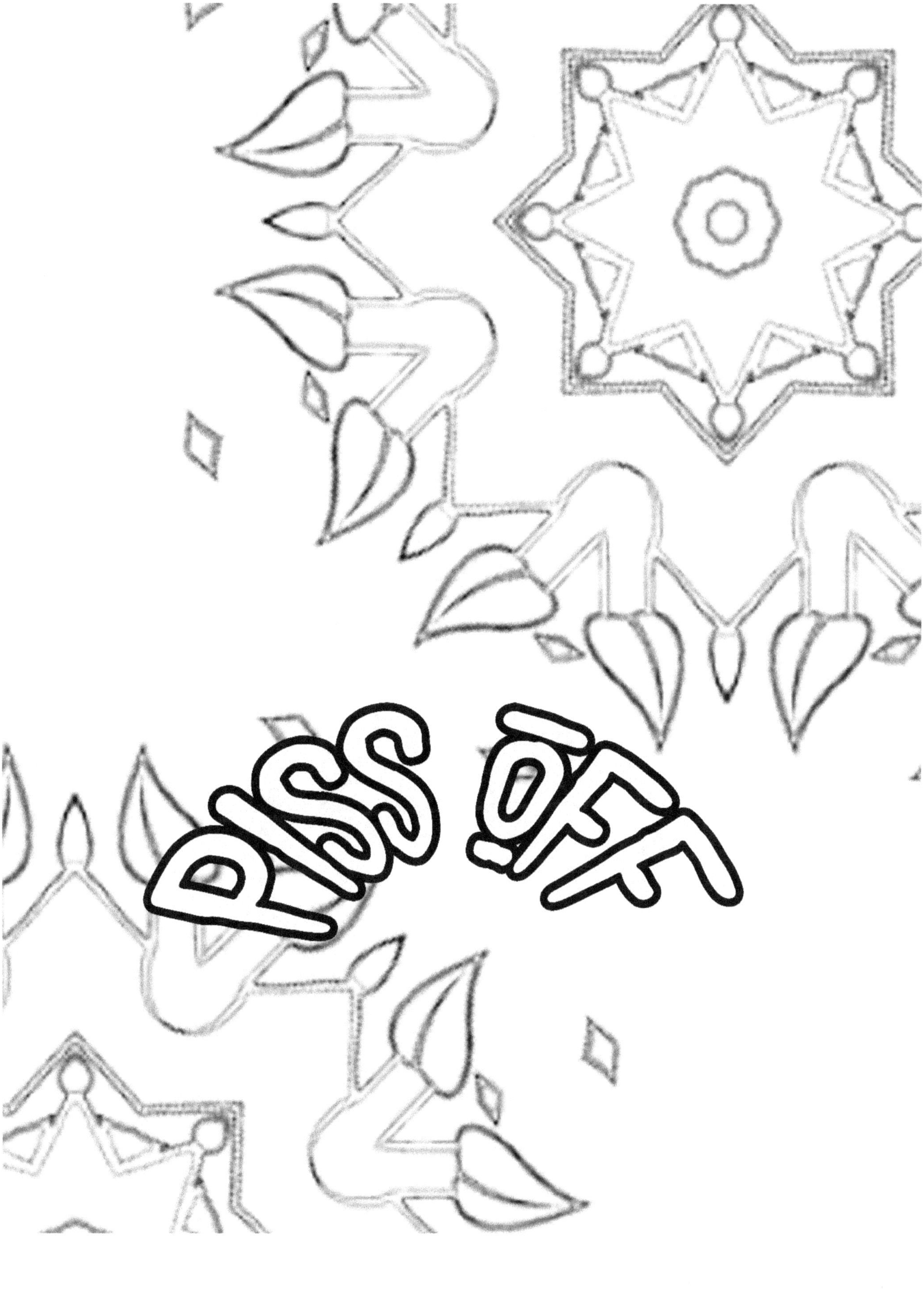
PISS OFF!

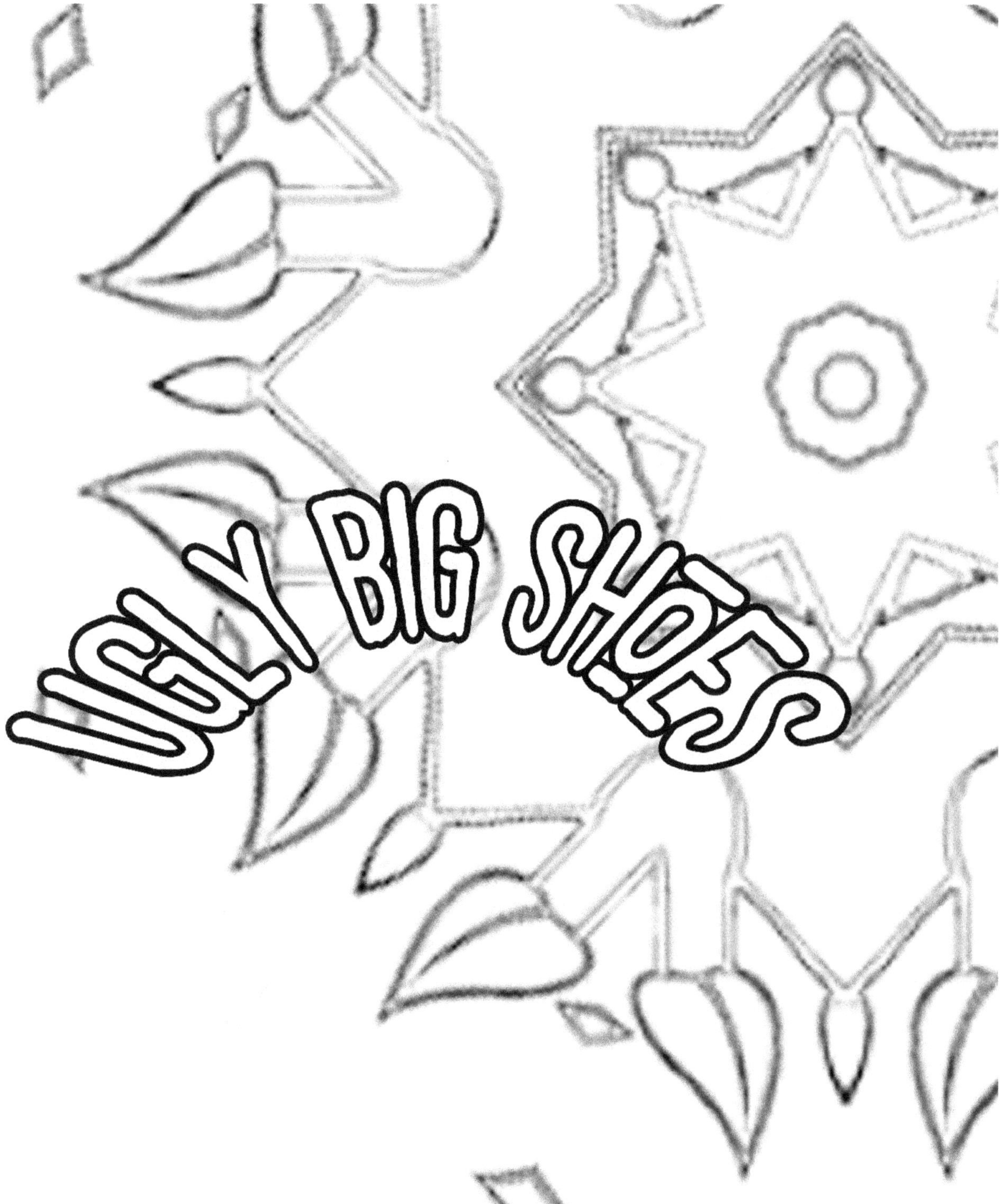
UGLY BIG SHOES

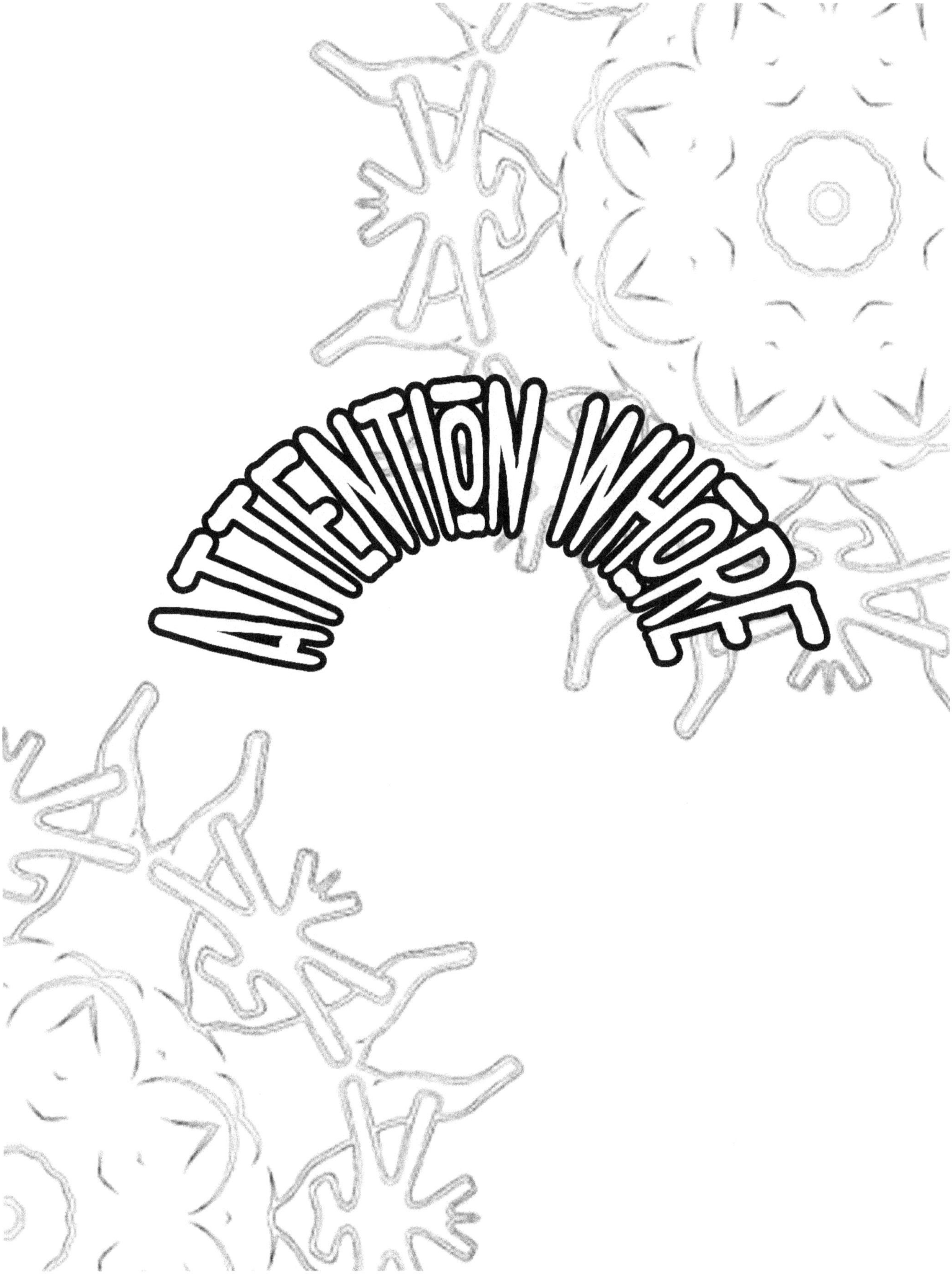
ATTENTION WHORE

www.ingramcontent.com/pod-product-compliance
Lightning Source LLC
Chambersburg PA
CBHW081742170526
45167CB00009B/3912
* 9 7 8 1 5 4 2 8 2 4 6 3 7 *